5

Who Works at a Library?

Do you have a question?

Ask a librarian! She helps

people find information.

A librarian orders new books,

music, and videos.

Do you want to borrow a book?

A library assistant can help!

She helps people sign up for

library cards. She checks out

books and answers the phone.

Who is in charge of a library?
The library director! He makes
plans and hires workers.
He makes sure everyone
does their jobs.

Look at all the books!

They need to be put away.

A worker places them on

the correct shelves. This worker

is called a library page.

Libraries are busy places!
Lots of people use the library
every day. A custodian keeps
the library clean.

How People Can Help

Volunteers help librarians. They put away books and read at story time. They plant flowers outside the library. Maybe you can help at your library!